Pam Scheunemann

Consulting Editor, Diane Craig, M.A./Reading Specialist

ABDO
Publishing Company

Published by ABDO Publishing Company, 8000 West 78th Street, Edina, Minnesota 55439.

Printed in the United States.

Editor: Katherine Hengel
Content Developer: Nancy Tuminelly
Cover and Interior Design and Production: Oona Gaarder-Juntti, Mighty Media
Photo Credits: ShutterStock

Library of Congress Cataloging-in-Publication Data

Scheunemann, Pam, 1955-
  Dogs bark! / Pam Scheunemann.
    p. cm. -- (Animal sounds)
  ISBN 978-1-60453-570-9
  1. Dogs--Juvenile literature. I. Title.

SF426.5.S32 2009
636.7--dc22
                          2008033920

SandCastle™ Level: Transitional

SandCastle™ books are created by a team of professional educators, reading specialists, and content developers around five essential components—phonemic awareness, phonics, vocabulary, text comprehension, and fluency—to assist young readers as they develop reading skills and strategies and increase their general knowledge. All books are written, reviewed, and leveled for guided reading, early reading intervention, and Accelerated Reader® programs for use in shared, guided, and independent reading and writing activities to support a balanced approach to literacy instruction. The SandCastle™ series has four levels that correspond to early literacy development. The levels are provided to help teachers and parents select appropriate books for young readers.

Emerging Readers	Beginning Readers	Transitional Readers	Fluent Readers
(no flags)	(1 flag)	(2 flags)	(3 flags)

SandCastle™ would like to hear from you. Please send us your comments and suggestions.
sandcastle@abdopublishing.com

Some dogs are big, and some are small.

The Great Dane is one of the largest dog breeds. The Chihuahua is the smallest.

3

It is hard not to love them all!

Dalmatians are born pure white. Their spots appear as they get older.

Dogs bark happily when they jump and run.

They play with toys and have some fun!

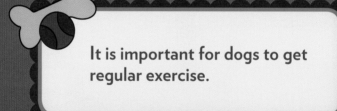

It is important for dogs to get regular exercise.

It is good to teach dogs to obey.

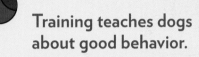

Training teaches dogs about good behavior.

You can train them to sit down and stay!

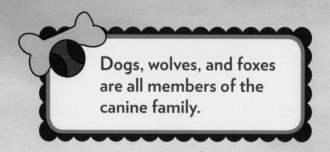

Dogs, wolves, and foxes are all members of the canine family.

Dogs can learn how to play fetch.

In fetch, a person throws an object such as a ball or a stick. The dog chases the object and then brings it back.

Sometimes dogs just want to stretch.

Most dogs like to take car rides.

Parked cars heat up very quickly, even if the windows are open. It is very dangerous to leave your dog in a parked car on a hot day.

Special dogs can act as guides.

Guide dogs are trained to help people who have disabilities.

Dogs bark in the morning and in the afternoon. Sometimes at night they howl at the moon!

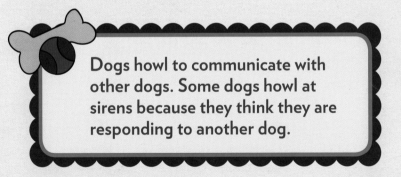

Dogs howl to communicate with other dogs. Some dogs howl at sirens because they think they are responding to another dog.

Glossary

breed (p. 3) – a group of animals or plants that have ancestors and characteristics in common.

canine (p. 12) – of or relating to dogs.

communicate (p. 23) – to share ideas, information, or feelings.

disability (p. 20) – the lack of ability, power, or fitness to perform certain tasks.

imitate (p. 24) – to copy or mimic someone or something.

respond (p. 23) – to reply or answer.

siren (p. 23) – a device that makes a loud, squealing sound as a signal or warning.

stretch (p. 16) – to extend something out to its full length.

Animal Sounds Around the World

Dogs sound the same no matter where they live. But the way that humans imitate them depends on what language they speak. Here are some examples of how people around the world make dog sounds:

English – woof woof
German – wau wau
Japanese – wan wan
French – ouah ouah
Greek – gav gav
Spanish – guav

To see a complete list of SandCastle™ books and other nonfiction titles from ABDO Publishing Company, visit www.abdopublishing.com.

8000 West 78th Street, Edina, MN 55439 • 800-800-1312 • fax 952-831-1632